ALL ABOUT

Eggs

And How They Change Into Animals

BY *Millicent Selsam*

ILLUSTRATED BY *Helen Ludwig*

Young Scott Books

Copyright © MCMLII by Millicent Selsam
All Rights Reserved
A Young Scott Book
Addison-Wesley Publishing Company, Inc.
Reading, Massachusetts 01867
Library of Congress Catalog Card No. 52-7272
ISBN: 0-201-09101-1
Printed in the United States of America

WZ/WZ   09101   10/75

Eggs, eggs, eggs! White eggs, speckled eggs, tremendous eggs, tiny eggs. Eggs with hard shells and with soft jelly coverings.

How different they are from each other. And no wonder! Because different kinds of eggs grow into different kinds of animals.

These are the eggs we know best.
If they hatch, what will come out?

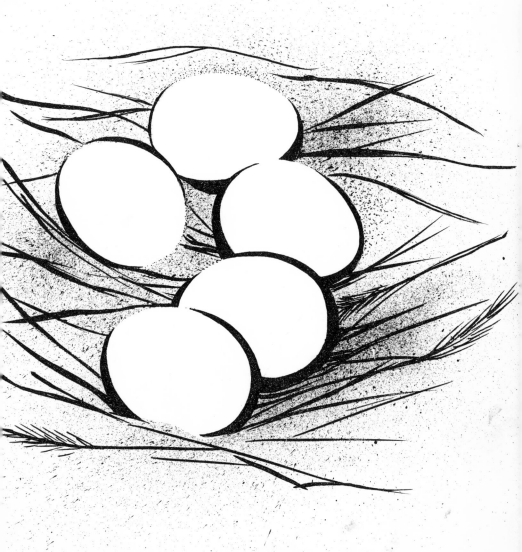

Baby chicks, of course.

Little fuzzy, yellow chicks that will grow up
into big hens and roosters.

Hundreds of thousands and millions of eggs!
That's what one single codfish lays.
What a crowd of codfish eggs are floating
here on the water.

Lots of these eggs will be gobbled up
by other fish that swim in the sea,
but . . .

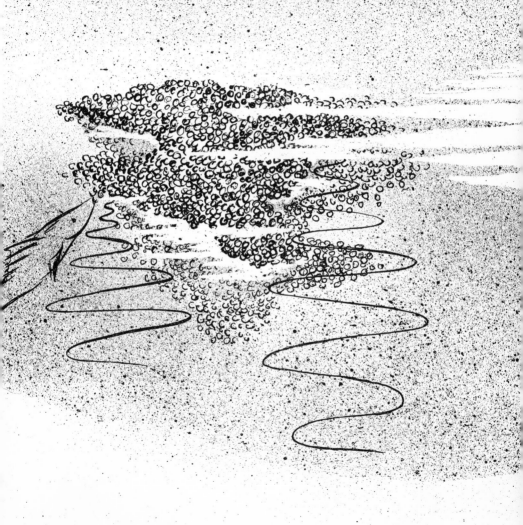

some of them will change into baby codfish and grow up into great big codfish.

Here are some white eggs with thin rubbery shells
lying in this hole.
They are in a nice warm sandy spot near a pond.
What will come out of these eggs?

**Tiny turtles will hatch from these eggs, march down
the muddy sides of the pond, and swim away in the water.**

There are only a few eggs
here in this nest
in a tree.
What's inside of these?

There are baby birds inside. They will peck at these shells
and crack them open . . . and out will come four baby robins.

There are eggs here, too, but tiny ones.
If you look closely you can see them
fastened to the bottom of the mother lobster.
She carries them around for almost a year.
You can guess what will hatch
from these eggs.

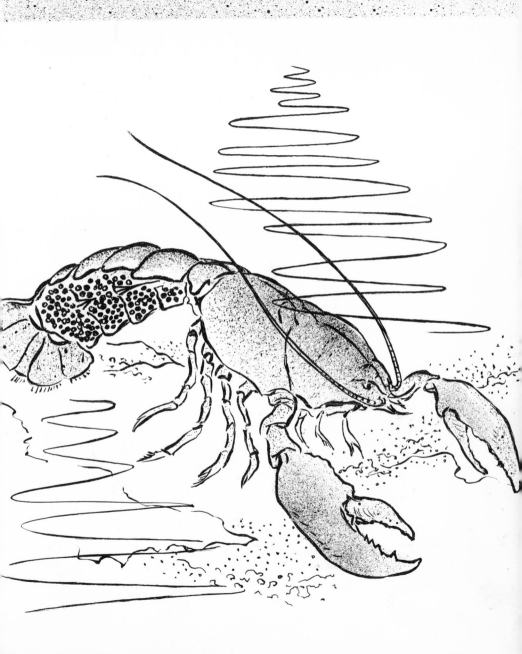

**Tiny baby lobsters will hatch out
and grow into the young lobsters you see here.**

Bees lay eggs, too.
But it isn't wise to peek
into a beehive
to see these eggs.
You might get stung!
But if you could see inside
you would find lots of eggs.
Each egg is in its own
little wax room.

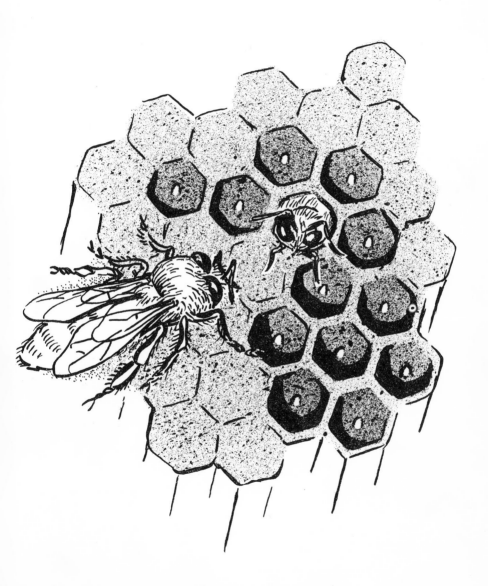

Each one will become a buzzing bee.

Here is a big lump of quivering jelly
in the middle of a pond.
There are hundreds of eggs inside.

First they will be tadpoles and then they will be frogs, hopping in and out of the very same pond.

These white eggs
with rough skins
will crack open
one day.
Can you guess
what will come
out of them?

Baby snakes—wriggly, little baby snakes!

Here are eggs—
great big eggs in a hole
in the dry sandy ground.
What will hatch out
of these tremendous eggs?

Nothing less than ostriches!

So many different kinds of eggs. Eggs in water, eggs in the sand. Rough eggs, smooth eggs, big eggs and little. They all come out of their mothers and are laid.

Then, outside of the mother's body, they break open their shells or coverings; and out come baby ostriches, or snakes, or frogs, or bees, or turtles, or chickens, or baby robins.

**Other animals have babies, too. But you never see their eggs at all.
Where are they?**

**A dog has babies,
but where are the dog's eggs?**

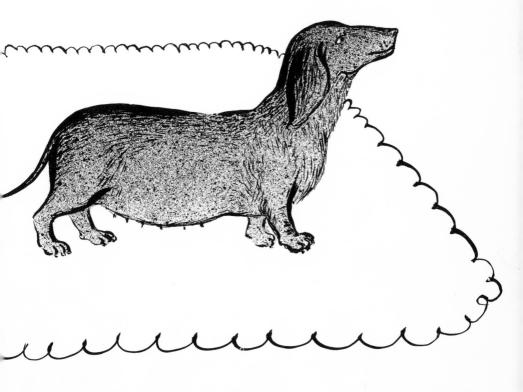

You don't see them but they are there just the same.
Hidden away inside the mother dog is a special sac—
a warm, safe place where the dog's eggs
change into little puppies.

And where are the cow's eggs?

**These eggs are hidden away, too. Inside the mother cow
is a sac where the cow's egg changes into a baby calf.**

And where are the whale's eggs?

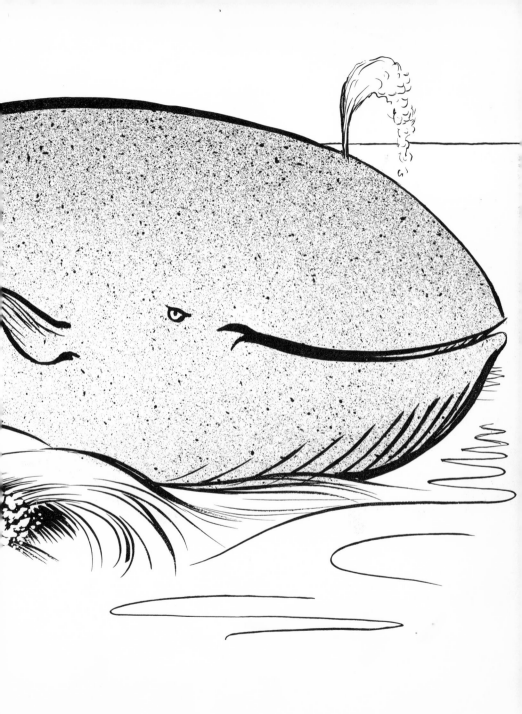

Inside the mother whale is the same kind of sac,
where the whale's egg changes into a baby whale.

And inside the mother cat, horse, sheep, giraffe, seal, pig,
and other animal mothers is the very same kind of sac
where their eggs change into babies.
They slowly grow and grow inside their mothers, until . . .

one day they come out into the world through a special tube
that stretches to let them out. They are born—
just as you yourself were born one day.

You, too, grew from a tiny egg inside your mother.

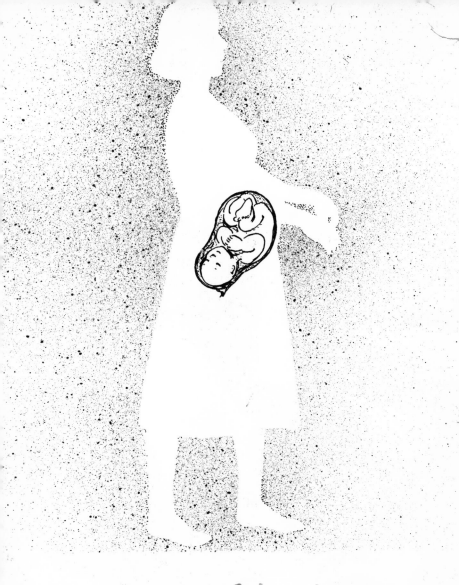

You, too, grew and grew until you were a full-sized baby ready to be born.